Inch Days

Poems and Paintings by Catherine Canning

GUILDHALL PRESS

Introduction

I have often been asked where ideas for my poetry come from. On Inch Island I took inspiration from the seasons, particularly lambing time, the return of the swallows to the shed, the habits of the badger and the comings and goings of the swans on the lake. From the landscape that quiets the mind, to the smells and the sights of the creatures that were less curious of me than I was of them. Many would dread the idea of standing in a freezing and draughty shed waiting for sheep to give birth; the blood, the smells, the chapped hands and cheeks. But for me it was an exciting experience to see steam rising from a new-born lamb or hear the cries of ewes struggling with a difficult birth.

There are many reasons why I write. One reason is that I have to. I am often compelled to put words on the page, as the poem *Death Before Birth* suggests: '. . . *words pour on my page like the dirty water I wash my hands in.*' Then I would move words about until they formed a picture or captured an event. For instance, as I tended the front garden of the small house I stayed at in Binalt, a garden laid down by a woman who lived all her life on Inch, thoughts would flood my mind, a word or a sentence that would come to me in the most common of activities.

I was touched by the experiences and the existence of those who had lived in this house before me. I felt the presence of a man, long gone, his stature still hovering in the shed amid the smells of damp and rusty nails. And on high shelves, his sister's things among her '. . . *hoard of delicate treasures*', two dusty porcelain dogs, now covered with cobwebs, which once decorated the mantle of a home now seen through my eyes. Thoughts of lives lived separate from me – a home, a place, an island people – all inspired me. I felt that recording their lives would make them live on in people's memories through my poetry.

As a poet and a painter I combine forces in the poem *Where Stillness Waits*: '*Stillness sighs, in awe of every thing that is beautiful. Blue paint brushes the sea with a wash of colour.*' My paintings, often primitive in style, evoke the simplicity of the island. I spent much of my time looking at the view: the changing sky and the ever-moving cloud formations; the surface of the sea, one day like glass, the next rough and wild; the distant hills, often blue, then grey, then brown. I felt compelled to paint them and it was there, in that house, that I first picked up a brush.

In this collection of my poetry and paintings I attempt to capture my love of nature, of Inch Island and the sense of belonging I felt while living there. Through the pages of this book I hope you, too, will be transported to another time, another place, a walk through my *Inch Days,* and linger a while to cherish where it takes you.

Catherine Canning

ISBN 978 1 906271 79 4

Copyright © Catherine Canning / Guildhall Press

Published in October 2013 by
Guildhall Press
Unit 15, Ráth Mór Business Park
Bligh's Lane, Derry BT48 0LZ
00 44 28 7136 4413
info@ghpress.com / www.ghpress.com

Cover image: Sweeneys' House, Binalt, Inch © Catherine Canning.

The author asserts her moral rights in this work in accordance with the Copyright,
Designs and Patents Act 1998.

A catalogue record for this title is available from the British Library.

Guildhall Press gratefully acknowledges the financial support of the Arts Council of Northern Ireland as a
principal funder under its Annual Funding Programme.

About the Author / Artist

Catherine Canning was born and educated in Nottingham, England, and is now resident between Derry and Inch Island, County Donegal. She graduated with a Bachelor of Arts in English Literature from the University of Ulster in 1993 and is a founding member of the Inch Writers' Group.

Catherine's short stories and poetry have appeared in various anthologies, including; *Passages* (Caldo Publications, 1985), *The Salmon* (Salmon Publishing), *Borderlines* (Holiday Projects West, 1988), and *Eve: A Celebration of Creative Women* (Guildhall Press, 2006). Her work has been broadcast on RTÉ Radio 1 and BBC Radio Foyle.

Awards include making the shortlist of the Bridport Poetry Prize 2009 and winning first prize for Best Collection of Poetry at the Charles Macklin Autumn School in 2006.

Catherine is a self-taught artist and has exhibited her work in County Donegal at the Charles Macklin Autumn School, Culdaff; Colgan Hall, Carndonagh; Kristof Gallery, Letterkenny, and The Glebe Gallery, Churchill. In Derry, Catherine has exhibited at The Void Gallery, London Street Gallery and The Shipquay Gallery of Fine Art. As a result of being runner-up in the Ulster Artist of the Year Award in 2009, Catherine had a solo exhibition in Café Artisan, Derry.

Acknowledgements

I would like to thank the Arts Council of Northern Ireland and Guildhall Press (Paul, Jenni, Joe, Kevin, Declan) for their support and professional advice; Emily, Harold and Kenneth Bryce; Frank Tormey; Mary Connors and the Inch Writers' Group and my family.

Special thanks are due to the following for allowing paintings from their private collections to be included in this publication:

Skart Rock – Marlene and Stephen Gallagher.

Trawling The Swilly – Deborah McGinn and Barry McDaid.

Inch Castle / John McGrath's / Wee House, Mill Bay – Maeve Doherty Holmes.

Through The Garden Gate – Patricia Norris.

Robb's Wee House – Pauline McKenzie.

Contents

For Louise and Barry,
Charlotte, Freya, Lennon and Bobby

John Sweeney

Rain spits in my face as I stand at his grave as though I had
every right to be there. Lead letters insecure to an
Inch Island wind lie face down on polished pebbles,
leaving pock holes on his faded headstone.

When I first turned the key in his lock
I met three ducks on the hall wall heading out,
but never getting beyond the front door.

I carried a box of chattering glasses to the shed
to wait beside his pots and cups,
and replaced them with my own.
Opening doors that he shut to let in draughts and neighbours.

I threw the lone armchair on its knees to beat out dust
and remnants of his rest: old currency hit lino and rolled for cover,
a friendless pen that wrote his lists and letters,
now lost for words. And matchsticks, long dead, fluff shrouded,
fell out of the trapped dark.

Wearied, I sit by the range,
where he sat years before rubbing the scales from his thick
red hands. The same cushion that held him back from work
moulds now to my shape, and above my head a speechless
clock hangs as though time fell asleep in this quiet house.

Counting Sheep

Turning my head to be sure I'm not being watched
I gawk at you in death; you are almost perfect in sleep
but your stomach lies open like a vacant boat,
balls of half-digested grass lie comfortably in the curved bowl,
your leg bone cleaned like polished teeth. A long black
slippery sac I mistook for a silk stocking lies close by.

Turquoise dye colours your neck, the mark of service.
I look closer at your face to see if you are recognisable
as Hogwart or Teddy Bear but I wouldn't know now,
your deep mustard eyes are gone, gorged by magpies.
I wondered who wolfed you first, who tore at your warm
wet wool, rat or fox.

The breeze is cut thin and scented by the sea, a brass-necked
gull hovers with ease in the air, I look up and see your sisters
watching me, closer now than they have ever allowed me to be,
some walk away, others follow but four or five stay defying me
and I'm glad of the company. We stand like friends at a wake
not wanting to leave, connected by standing in the rain,

connected by being female, connected by being alive.
As the heavens open, like the flies I move away,
leaving you in peace and climb the hill,
meaning to come back at dusk to continue the vigil,
if the farmer hasn't buried you before then.

Skart Rock

The Pheasant

Flies raise their noses in search of you, as you
lie in a fish box in the shed,
their heavy blue bodies drunk on your rich odour.
Do they feed on your dried blood
or lay eggs in your wounds?
I'll ask him if he comes.

Seeds not touched these three days now,
my car swallowed you up
on a bad bend, then spat you out bleeding
from shoulder and wing into a sucker's arms.
A black car slowed and laughed,
another directed me to a house.

'I'll give you two choices,' he said,
'a lot of bother or ring its neck.'
I never knew what bother meant.
After three days I lifted her
thinking she'd rested enough.

Bringing her to a sheltered spot
she flapped her wing awkwardly,
head banging the soft ground.
I carry her back to the fish box
blood painting my hands

from a freshly opened wound,
as her smell trails behind me.
I place her in the fish box and steal away,
while thick yellow liquid
runs down my leg,
icing the top of my new red shoes.

Blue Smoke

A labouring tractor moves
among mothers and babies
scattering air through a yellow bucket.
Inside he listens to the radio
turns the dial above his capped head.
Down to the sea and up to the hill
he moves, feeding a field.
Fine paper-blue smoke
opens to the sky
from a worn-out pipe,
it paints brightness
on the grey heavens.

Mountains In Mist

Two Dead Lambs

Prolapsed girl
wait and see
rope her up
or let her be
two dead lambs
hard to bear
cover your face
with nice clean hands
blood on straw
bright-blue string
on two black paws.

Plastic glove past your elbow
cold stale stench
to turn your stomach
in again
to find the other
another head in your hand
torn-faced lamb
dry as a bone
dead on straw
by five strong fingers
in a bloody glove.

Get that woman away from me
hand over mouth the smell of soap
bring my babies' bloody bodies
get your father to bring me water
call your mother to heat it up.

Should he
have left you to die?
she prayed for it
with her pressed clean hands
not my hands
I have blood on them
not my hands
I brought the water
not my hands
they're in my pockets.

Someone must know
who let her suffer?
who watched?
turn away quick
not my business
not my sheep
bring the graip
open the pit
join your hands
for two dead lambs.

April

The silence sits
heavy and muted as a snowdrift,
jackdaws high in the chimney
echo down the long pipe
to the click of a cooling range,
their housekeeping brings comfort.
Tired legs ache from a long walk,
the book on my lap fidgets
in folded fingers.
Knowing I have a wake to attend
my mind drifts there in dread.
Down at the stables
the man with the grey handlebars
lies in a cold conservatory,
his widow wishing him back
with sighs of, 'if only, if only...'

Inch In Snow

My Foot You Can't

I called you from a room full of company
because you were the closest to the door.
'Can you lift that black thing?' I said, 'but don't kill it.'
I watched you raise your boot,
I was about to repeat myself
when I heard its hard coated body crush

to the sound of clapping.
You lifted two oyster shells from the windowsill
and used them as reluctant undertakers,
a pink one peppered with barnacles
and another polished pearl
too much beauty for a task of death.

You scooped the shells together
and lifting the flattened insect
threw it out of the window.
At the door you turned and said,
'You can't recycle everything.'

Trying to save its life
but afraid it would be too quick for me
and run up my arm, I gave you the task as saviour
but you were an unwilling rescuer,
I was thinking it doesn't take much to kill a beetle
I could have done that myself.

I assumed a man who works the land
fourteen hours a day wouldn't be threatened
by an inch-long insect nor kill anything unnecessarily,
one who was heartbroken at finding lumps
in two of his favourite sheep,

who keeps two dogs; one for working, one for walking.
The next morning, coming in from feeding the hens,
I see it's still there on the outside of the window ledge.
I place it in the plant pot by the door, ashes to ashes,
dust to dust – who says I can't recycle everything?

The Badger

I carry a stack of buckets into the shadows of the shed,
the dog is beside himself with excitement. Something dark
is lying in the corner of the trailer, my little friend,
nut thief and mound mover at home in a tin. Like final tears;
twin streams of blood flow from its eyes, now breakfast for birds.
I knew sickness followed you for weeks like an unwanted flea,
now nature, as necessary as rain delivers you a contented corpse.
Hatless, he crossed the yard half-smiling to himself as though cheered

by some yarn or trick, I call and tell him.
'Aye, me da shot it,' he shouts in good humour.
I sit down on the tree stump, a stepping-stone to the trailer,
taking the weight off my weightless legs,
I have been bludgeoned and sucked dry.
In the yard where hoggets leave trays of unfinished nuts,
I hold on to a wet rusted gate and think about your windfall of getaways,
safer than a coconut at a fairground, the father gunning for you
in worn-out eyes as you tore up the yard.

Three square meals and more a boxcar diner, I saw you there
till the cows came home, enclosed spaces too dangerous for farmers
with guns, shrapnel to take an eye or chips at a cheekbone.
But pride, simmering like a festered boil under skin, determines
he'd not be made a fool of and he marked your card.
In no mood for work, I fold up, and pulling out
of the yard I see the back of his head
as he sits in his kitchen enjoying his breakfast.

Trawling The Swilly

Nest Building

I make nest boxes for blue tits
that he said were too neat.
I nail them high and furnish them;
a country seat for robins hangs hidden in ivy
sheltered like a new perm.
A disused glove drawer,
roofed now,
bracketed sloppily to a bruised lintel
becomes a squat for starlings.
Waiting and watching,
with too much love and hope
only jackdaws come,
making lonely sounds
they squawk at me
from a high chimney.

The Old Shed

In the old shed, their lives are stored
where wardrobes stand tall and lonely.
Their mirrors laced with cobwebs,
they hold no ghosts of memory –
all vacant of images of Sunday bests
of those who fixed a hat
or flicked fluff from a chipped shoulder.
A heavy black range, it took four men to lift,
is tired standing under a broken window, a coming
and going passage for a high-tailed wren typing protest songs.

In a kitchen press, to the rapid run of mildew, woodlice raise families
and claim squatters' rights among her ornaments;
a silver tankard, harp clad, unengraved, seems out of place –
too harsh, too masculine, a tarnished bully hidden
among her best things. A hoard of delicate treasures
to brighten dull days – a delf bear, a seaside souvenir;
cheap and hollow with empty promises.

Now years of settled dust dull her best-kept brass.
In behind her matching dogs, her holy pictures and plastic flowers,
good plates and cups reserved for visitors that mostly let her down.
Under a dripping roof sits her big tin pot,
for soup days and stew days and never-got-away days,
a good brown bowl for baking and jars in boxes kept for autumn jam.

A rolled mat rests on a chest of drawers that never held
the treasures of her bottom drawer just practical things;
blouses and slips, vests and knickers, some kept for good or best.
A Christmas nightdress, a parcelled gift from a Glasgow cousin,
a lemon cardigan; too good for going nowhere.
And smaller drawers – swollen with damp and festered secrets.
A broach, and beads she never got to wear, stockings,
an odd glove – the other dropped, brought disappointments,
or bad luck, or no luck. Just long browned-off Sundays
and too much work for two bachelor brothers,
and herself, that would bring shame on the family,

sent by boat to birth a baby boy she never did bring home,
her cup of love she never got to give, just a growing grief
that got her in the end.
They sat out their end of days in a tiny kitchen
you couldn't swing a cat in.
Newspapers stacked as high as their hopes,
from floor to ceiling leaving little room to sit,
filling their space with things they kept a lifetime;
things they would never need,
content with less than they deserved,
starved of untold surprises.

The Old Shed

A Tap At The Window

She walked to the wee shed.
Nine hens, one rooster and two ducks followed her
they thought she was the source.
Their container was empty
not a grain left to give them.

Back at the new house she searched the cupboards –
flour, sugar, tinned stuff.
In the bread bin she found a packet of
damp Tuck biscuits,
she read the packet, 'fourteen grams of salt'.

She put her foot on the pedal-bin and threw them in.
She heard a tap at the window
and looked up to see four hens sitting on the windowsill,
she put her arm deep into the dirty bin,
no need for salt on eggs tomorrow.

John McGrath's

Sheep Song

Overdressed for April, they house their heavy coats
like armour, gossiping in the shade of a sycamore
while their lambs are left to run riot.

Daisies hunger for spring in short grass, stretching their
white fingers in the heat, sunshine moves like a skater,
graceful and flawless across the top field.

Beyond the road, workmen get ready to rest tools at the end
of a long day, the cement mixer slows
like a record on a wound-up gramophone.

In the yard the rooster sits nervously beside a meowing cat,
a pied wagtail worries that her new-built nest has been misplaced,
she watches the cat stretch and cross the yard.

High in a tree a collared dove coos for its dinner, his mate feathers
her nest for eager eggs, coming any day soon.
Sparrows squabble in the hedges

as the cat lies down again under the bird table and waiting begins.
Back in the field sheep move their youngsters
to higher ground for evening will soon be drawing in over the lough.

Bogwood

Their grey corpses stand like trophies in hard peat.
Dried, broken and bleached at the sun's mercy
their bones stand upright, roots long dead
hold tight to the knitted mat of bog,

as though some present mystery still lives on in them.
Diggers with plans for new homes uproot them
leaving them exposed and
naked on the earth's surface.

Their limbs broken
their strong backs hunched in hunger,
their shapes still forming
by the wind's sharp cut.

Their proud and tragic history talks to me,
their beauty even in death moves me.
I mourn their lost life long before I came,
when for centuries they rested in peace.

Photo Album

You gatecrashed our viewing past and joined us confidently
to see me in that mustard top I always loved,
in big-eyed sunglasses my head stuck in a book,
you would never have known me, you said. We laughed
at my First Communion, wearing a toothless grin,
head to the side shyly, crooked veil nesting on a home perm.

A prayer book open in folded fingers, my bitten nails
disguised in black and white. And Grandfather on a grey day,
his face brightening Grianan Fort, back turned
on the Swilly view, me in a green coat, wind parting my hair.

And then the studio portrait of a toddler with a pet lip,
holding a powder puff my aunt gave me,
to keep me quiet beside my sister in ringlets.
Next, all steps and stairs squeezed into a sofa, in shabby clothes
and freshly washed faces, posing for that door-to-door photographer.
Me in front, holding the baby too tight, the grubby wall marked

with dirty hands; that, and being part of a big family,
embarrassed me. I closed it shut, leaving lives leather bound
in faded red. When she rose to go inside
I wanted you gone before she refilled her glass
but still you stayed kicking the dirt in your old boots.

Swilly View

Where Stillness Waits

While the palm tree rattles her fingers
against a warm breeze,
a wren types a love letter in the distance
and I dig up jam jars in the front garden.

Behind me, a cool draught
stones my neck
while one cheek reddens
with the warmth of the sun.

Across the lough a startled schooner
shuts off its engine, in the moment,
I catch my breath,
waiting for nothing to move.

Stillness sighs,
in awe of everything that is beautiful.
Blue paint brushes the sea
with a wash of colour.

On my table, a fly walks miles
across my clean blank page,
it exhausts me, I exhale,
time starts again.

Gone Fishing

The Visitor

When you arrived, I was on my knees,
painting black-eyed susans
on an old fish box; a summer bed for marigolds,
your blue car crawling up the lane.

I watched your laboured task; of switching bottles,
your sucking in, your blowing out.
I rise, unsure and uneasy,
you call to me, 'Keep on with what you're doing.'

Carrying your bottle of breath,
the tube feeding your nose
you walk towards me smiling,
the film playing in my head stars
another *Pop* and *daughter dearest*
hugging, in soft and cushioned comfort.

Later I stood in the kitchen waiting
for a stubborn kettle to boil,
outside the window sweet pea,
stingy with its perfume, grows in a Belfast sink.

I carry a tray into the yard
the rattle of tea cups calling hens,
they fan their greed with excitement
running after me.

I cut the cake you brought
while you sit, shade cooled,
shovelling sugar into your cup.
Planes paint white lines in a busy sky
anticipating the Atlantic.

Then you repeat the story of how your mother
kept coal and a clocking hen
in the cubby-hole under the stairs,
while the rest scratched a living
in the concrete yard.

You talk of a happy childhood
that might have been,
of walking miles from Donegal
to leave girls home from dances
when fathering twelve was
a mystery yet to be revealed.

At four you left,
heat still withering seedlings in the shade.
I crumbed the cake I couldn't eat
and fed it to the hens.
Returning to the kitchen
I caught a whiff of scent
through the grey net curtain
waving in a welcome breeze.

Being Watched

I leave a city of night violence,
constant traffic, queues by wheel and foot,
telephones ringing for favours and who's that
at the door, for a country croft with little to do,
heavy with silence, noisy with birdsong.

Carrying buckets of weeds for dumping
and clay for pots of colour,
as she might carry shopping,
buying must-haves to happiness
to push into swollen cupboards
of more *buy-one-get-one-free*
and hardwares full of good intentions
all used-up time and petrol.

Here a peace enfolds, where the sky
is vast with grey or blue,
yet I'm of no more importance
than a random stone on a high hill.
But I stumble in my solitude
to see a camera spying on me
from a wooden pole, at the foot
of a redundant road,
someone is watching me
doing nothing, going nowhere.

Wee House, Mill Bay

The Rat

The yard is spread out, bare-chested, grass-tufted,
its edges lined with daffodil yellow,
open mouthed, their golden trumpets
hum to the music of bees.

I keep a keen eye for last week's visitor
seeking bread and friendship,
he came out when the sky was ocean blue, deep and cold:
only a delicate sun took the sharpness off *that* cruel day.

Now he's back, skulking in sunlight, brave and brassy brown,
right in the middle of the yard.
Heat clicks the tin roof calling his welcome,
no shadow or debris hides him.

My pages flap in the breeze and he stays
watching me with black pearl eyes,
his hunched back unwelcome words,
his front claws turning bread like a silver sixpence.

In the sycamore, a robin cautions him over territory,
above her, stripped branches finger-point to the sky:
like skeletons, they rattle their bare bones
to the music of an easterly wind.

The sea pours noise in my ear,
startled, he scarpers,
full of a feast of wheaten,
hopping and skipping like a child in a playground.

My skin crawls to a pair of brown leaves
playing tag too close for comfort,
the brush of the tablecloth
against my leg unnerves me.

By the hen-house door, his tail turns a curtain of green,
bluebells, still blind,
stroke his fur with their long fingers,
he runs towards me giddy with courage.

I stand, he stays, and I steal away, back watching,
carrying fear like a black secret.
Only the blue hard cake of poison will stop him
but I'll keep my hands clean.

A review will come in April when hens rule the yard
when his footprints stain my satin eggs,
and I hear him run for cover in the coop
hair crawling my neck like an itchy blanket.

Lovesick Blue Tit

His droppings, acrylic white,
eat the body of my car,
he taps for hours on end
wooing his lovely unreal
mate in my side-view mirror.

I'll fix him a mirror
by the nut feeder
for he should come and eat.
I coax him like a worried mother,
tie fat balls to an s-shaped hook,
secure the mirror to the post and wait.

Now, no birds feed.
They fear a rival who doesn't come
till they come
and doesn't leave till they leave.
In the end, I remove it –
leave nature to nature.

Like a caged budgie
lonely for a mate
he taps his heart out.
If he doesn't hurry
he'll miss his chance,
she'll be swept off her feet in the last dance.

Rathmullan

Last Wishes

You threw your aunt away today.
She asked for Fr Hegarty's Rock but you're all
too old, you say, to walk that far. She went
over the Crana Bridge instead.
Remind me not to ask you when it's my turn to go
for I'm heading for Binalt.

My son has promised to talk nice
to Mr Rodgers, for I want to be thrown in the yard,
to be scratchings for hens, constantly on the move.
I've watched them dust their feathers in the dirt
on warm days, I'll take that,
that way I could live forever.

I was thinking if my son emigrates
to Australia you could do the job
but I've had a change of heart,
for when talking of your aunt you said
you would have to relocate the scatter…

somewhere close to a car park
and I'm having none of it.
Looks like the only way to get the job done right
is to do it myself.

A Bucket Of Nuts

On a Sunday before church you came to feed
the sheep, a daily task in February,
you crossed the field and all the girls ran after you.
The wind was fog coloured and razor sharp
mapping my cheeks with thin rivers of blood;
like a weather-beaten old hag in old clothes,

bearded and warted I ran to watch you, feeling foolish.
Standing on grass chewed short as a crew cut
I shifted and shuffled around you, getting in the way
while you forked silage into a framed blue barrel
sliced sideways, a breakfast bowl for ewes.
The pungent meal caught my breath like sour vinegar

on soggy chips. 'Young Kain Hutchinson could smell that
all day long!' you shouted laughing and I moved closer
and caught the sound of soft classical music playing
on a tractor radio; a comfortable piece
made for warm sitting rooms with soft lights,
wandering now, out of place in the cold field.

Sheep guzzled while you counted them: one missing
you move off and climb the hill to look for her,
'She has a prolapse,' you told me,
'I'll have to push it in and rope her.'

Bending low I inspected her like a bleary-eyed drunk,
sprung from her oversized rump, sprouted a
bulbous ball, like kidneys choked in cling film.

Later you came back to take her away. Grabbing her
thick coat, you pulled her to the box; her insides trailing
behind her, she lay down and refused to get up,
you handed me a bucket. While your back was turned
I stroked her coarse white face and hoped she wouldn't

bleed to death. Then you were both gone
and I was left holding the bucket of nuts
you gave me and I felt ashamed at the excitement
of knowing that later, when I crossed the field,
all the girls would run after me.

Mist In The Top Field

Staying Late

It is a treat, this staying late,
watching the street quieten,
hearing the rain fall.
Everything else gone,
no cars, no footsteps,
even the fire has gone,
the charcoal log stopped clicking,
her cooling silent.
The taste of loneliness in my mouth
is sweet like honey.
The wind whispering in the distance
rocks the high-street lamp,
the yellow light sways,
the street rocks sideways
like a happy drunk, still
grinning from the last laugh.
I will not look at the clock
nor worry at the lateness of the hour,
I will read and write and drink tea
and stay up all night
and not be sorry,
till tomorrow.

Lonesome Hens

Hens search the field
for the company of sheep
but they're gone now,
closer to the house to lamb,
to be set free on February mornings
into weak sunshine and
fed nuts twice a day from long trays.
And when their time comes
they will spread their weight
in the shelter of the shed,
where straw will take the chill off a concrete floor.

For hens in Binalt the day is long
and the place lonely without them,
they cluck-clucked under
wet swollen bellies
and found comfort there.
From a high tractor he was heard to say,
'They'll be back in four weeks, six at the most,'
while nine brown hens walked away cluck-clucking,
shaking their heads.

The Waiting Room

The waiting room
is the nursing room
that you waited a long time to get into,
waiting for someone to die.

Now you wait
for someone to dress you,
then wait at a table
for breakfast,
reading cracks in an empty cup,
your arthritic finger
painting over a pattern.
Waiting.

Waiting to be taken back to your room
to wait,
waiting for your tablets,
for someone to take you to the toilet
before you wet yourself
now waiting for someone to change you.

Waiting for visitors
and tea
and a drink of water,
waiting to be put to bed.
Waiting.

Now others are waiting, too,
in a queue,
waiting for you to die
so they can have your room
and join in the waiting.

Through The Garden Gate

The Tracker

For Patrick and Denise

A thin-sliced moon calls me from a warm house,
the night is full of promise.
I crunch stones in heavy boots,
all noise gives way to my trespass.
Holding down a tussling coat to a busy wind,
deep glass holes trick me as I paddle into their open mouths.
Earlier in sunlight I was the great tracker;
the great Indian stalker discovering hoof prints
freshly stamped on the even face of a mudpack.

Then, high excitement paved the way for greater disappointment
but I would not be told, walking out
alone through rugged ground seeking deer.
My human noise ran in front of me like a squeaky wheelbarrow.
Shushing myself as I ploughed on,
all wildlife heard me coming
long before I was seen,
in a warm and practical sky-blue hat.

Hours later my sore knees carry me home,
the light in the sky was a low-watt bulb.
Across the lake and high in the hills
I hear an unfamiliar cry,
it battles with the wind for my attention.
On the other side of this world a dog barks in answer,
something is somewhere else tonight and I tread
my disappointment in heavy boots,
back to a warm house.

Death Before Birth

Your spade slices the soft earth
that stands shivering like chocolate cake,
then falls to the cut of a steel blade.
You climb out of the hole fit now
for a child's coffin, straight walled, accurate and cold.

When you throw her in she lands awkwardly,
legs stiff as posts, you jump back in and position
her, fit for comfort, eyes still open,
watching but not seeing,
the late afternoon follows her into the darkness.

You ask did I say a *Hail Mary*
but I had said my prayers for her as I hunkered
beside her in the shed, holding her square coarse
face in my hands, praying she could hold on.

The smell smothering us as you pulled
the dead lamb from her, she called in pain
as humans do but the third was too much for her
and she lay blood-stained and stiff
against the cold concrete wall.

I rose to get the graip, lifted her babies,
bloated and heavy, carried them
one by one to the pit, the third was blue,
belly veined he came with his own sac of blood,
the stain followed me across the yard.

I threw the tin lid aside and dropped them in,
stood back, staring for the first time
at a pitful of death. Infant death,
mothers go to another plot,
buried side by side in Anderson's field.
These people carry no grief, their mind is set on
vet bills and the rising cost of feed,
death before birth is never counted; to live then die is a bigger loss.

Now, here at my table, miles away,
words pour on the page like the dirty water
I washed my hands in, thrown across the yard.
Yet I still smell the dead, the rotting flesh,
a reminder of her struggle, her lambs and her death.

Slate House

Home

Her home is a cluttered burrow
and she doesn't want to go there.
The ash of dead paper keeps falling,
stacks of envelopes for recycling,
books on shelves too high to reach,
boxes of photographs not good enough for albums
and bills and bills for shredding.

Her home is full of a thousand things
she will never use, or might
if she could find them.
They wait, gathering dust.
Stuff of hobbies and fortunes to be made;
beneath blank canvasses and hardened paint,
sit boxes of folded cloth, and a sewing machine
that waits for her,
that *has hands for anything*.

Mountains of cards to wish you Christmas Greetings,
cards for Paddy's day and Easter day
and new-baby day.
All stacked, all waiting, all dying,
all falling as dust.
So she ran away to the hills,
where the quiet of Dunlewey
folded in on her.

Sitting still, in a white house:
white walls, white chairs, clear cleaned glass.
Where dust is hard to find,
and fresh-made beds
settle in the comfort of ironed sheets.
Curtains tucked with counted folds,
hang open-winged to sunlight.

In a spotless kitchen,
counter-tops are cleared of clutter,
cupboards spoilt for space house,
four cups, four plates, three pots, one pan.
Vacant of stuff she didn't need
but thought she did.

The day is coming soon
when she'll go back to her cluttered burrow
And think of Larkin's line –
'Home is so sad. It stays as it was left.'
But she longs to find it,
not as it was left;
the breakfast bowl still by the sink,
the lilies dead in the vase,
the ashes settled in the grate,
the air stale, the dust thicker.

Cousins

Once upon a time there were
two little princesses
who often changed their names
and one cold winter's day they went
with the queen to a little house in Inch.
When they got tired

they played apart in the dim room,
each in their own little world.
The younger played a silent game of serving,
a tray of spoons and empty cups leading the way,
blanket over her head,
a red bride of Christ.

The bigger one, sofa bound,
looked down
and frowned at the spectacle,
sailing her long ship of isolation
she refused to speak,
clothing her quietness secretly.

Each with their own imaginings,
they moved further apart
into the shadows of the cooling room.

Mill Bay

Isy Darling

Finding no-one in the family to put her up
we took her to Donegal, from Thailand
or Cambodia or some other paradise she came.
We each trailed our long shadows
along an empty beach, posing for photographs
that did us no justice. But as the evening

wore on with laughs, then tiredness,
her spirit surrendered to the mellow
effects of wine and I watched her grab
door frames for balance, coming back
in from inhaling roll-ups.
She laughed, then cried, then laughed again,
recalled taking her five-year-old sister
to Piggery Ridge to see her heartthrob soldier.

She was fifteen when she ran away to London,
three days later her best friend was tarred and feathered.
'Drinking champagne on yachts with the best of people,
who call me *Isy darling*,
is what I do these days,' I heard her say, as
I eavesdropped by a sink of dirty dishes,
way past my bedtime, listening to them
talking and laughing outside,
their raised voices ruining the silent night.

They told me I was missing
all the craic being a non-smoker,
the insider, in a tiny kitchen, longing for bed,
while they sniggered and repeated themselves.

In the morning, waiting for her to rise,
I drank tea and read yesterday's news
and watched birds search for breakfast
in a cold spring wind.
At eleven I went in to wake her before the
best of the day was gone. I found her still asleep,
a wide-eyed doll in her arms.

In A Glass House

Here he sits,
coffee comforted,
in a glass house
while the world roars.
Wind attacks on all sides,
trees are beaten senseless.

Over there,
hens stay in,
a stream runs through their house,
their feet stay wet all day.

Outside,
he braves the gale,
to give them extra feed,
even though they don't belong to him.

From the nest
he lifts two eggs,
puts them deep in a blue pocket,
even though they don't belong to him.

The wind,
pushes him fast
down a slippery path,
an empty bucket beats against his leg,
he worries about eggs
deep in a blue pocket.

Back,
in the comfort of the glass house,
he lights the lamp too early
and thinks about staying the night.

In this draught-free house
the howling gale
pushes itself against glass.
In the distance white horses gallop
on the sea's bumpy surface.

The dark,
is moving in
across the Swilly,
rain washes the windows clean
outside the glass house.

Inch Castle

Still Waiting

'I'm staying for the moon,' she said,
when we rang looking for a lift back to Derry.
Days, weeks, months she's waited to see a badger.
'You'll see one for sure at full moon,' they said.
So she stayed for the moon.

She sneaked into the gallery to take her seat
followed by a pest of a cat that could cry for Ireland.
The stage is swept, the lights are lit,
badgers waited in the wings, she held her breath
any minute now –
an aimless elbow hit the switch,

the Gods turned their heads in slow motion,
the Divine plan had been sabotaged
no-one saw it coming.
Too late – black ink spilled across the moon,
a shower of stars sighed with disappointment. The sky

turned black; wind on its way through the sycamore
dropped to the weeds on the dirt road
like rats scurrying for cover.
With head drooped she trudged back to the house,
in a green nightdress and wellies
followed by a cat that is still crying for Ireland.

The Home That Wasn't Mine

I was dropped off at the bottom of Bowarran and told now walk home as if it were a punishment and although it seemed like a good idea at the time I wasn't having fun I tried to appreciate the blue in the sky and all the new growth and the birds singing and the sheep baaaaaing but I couldn't so I called in on Stan and he was painting his garden table white and he was shuffling about in his slippers and in his old clothes dripping paint everywhere and it was hard to watch and his fat cat sniffed my leg just in case and I pretended to love it and he turned the table on its side to paint the legs and the top that was already wet got dirty and I told him he should have painted the legs first and he said I know and it was hard to watch and when we ran out of things to talk about I said I'd go and he said away you go but hold on and come on in till you see this and he called me into the dark house to show me his cooker that he'd painted earlier and I said grand job so he gave me a mug and it was a nice thing because he bought it in London years ago 'cause I said I only had cups back at the house and I don't like drinking out of cups so I thanked him and left and started for home again and two lost sheep ran ahead of me on the road and I kept trying to get in front of them to let them into a field and any field would have done and sure anyone with any sense knows you wouldn't get in front of sheep on a narrow road unless you grew wings and I tried to enjoy the blue sky and all the new growth and forget about the sheep but I couldn't 'cause one of them was limping badly and I felt sorry for her so I couldn't enjoy my walk and eventually they ran up Mary Green's driveway to eat her good plants and I hurried on home only it wasn't really my home

Dunlewey

In memory of Hester Baldrick

How can, where she is gone
be better than this,
the sky bluer,
the place coated with colour?

How can, the sun be kinder,
the lake brim more with life,
the breeze calmer,
the lark fly higher
and sing a louder song?

Here, I am folded
in a Donegal light,
where the nearness of the wind
plays with my listening.
Everything else is bathed in stillness.
In the silence of my human poverty
I listen for God's consolation.
But that is my want,
my human expectation.

God is, when my spirit
is touched by these surroundings,
when I hear Him in the wind,
His breath blow clouds across the sky,
brushing the bronze hills with shadow.
He is in the waiting blueness of the sky,
in the green of the forest,
in the life, deep in the lake.

It is here, in all these things,
that He speaks to me,
Even now, He is coming towards me,
in the movement of the bog grass,
in the sway of the heather
that has yet to bloom.

Heading Away

Wet Sunday

The sky has been sobbing since yesterday. I had been listening
to *Desert Island Discs* and it exhausted me.
David Attenborough at eighty-six doesn't get tired just knee pain,
the statement floored me. After the theme tune I crawl to bed, ashamed,
but try not to feel ashamed.

Before he started I thought he'd be a jazz and classical man.
I was wrong about the jazz, he picked one similar to Strauss
only not Strauss, he said he could listen to it on his tropical island
when he was not in good spirits. I thought he was always in good spirits.
I scolded myself for not being in good spirits.

He came from a family of three boys till his mother brought home
two Jewish girls during the war and then there were five.
She told him to stop complaining and to be grateful
he had a mother and father; unlike them. They stayed four years.
I think he was glad when they left for America.

In bed, tears wash the skylight window,
trees bend and peer in at me
their nosiness unsettles me
as though they want to know
why am I in bed at this time of day on a wet Sunday.

Joan Baez is singing to me, she wrote this song with her son,
the thought disturbs me, why can't I write songs with my son,
why can't I just write songs?
In the end I get up, throwing the duvet over Joan Baez,
and go downstairs to find my wellies.

That Derry One

I want to be remembered as
the woman who taught her how to draw vases,
and pushed her high on the makeshift swing
when she was eight, her long hair
brushing the big leaves of the sycamore,
while the rope clicked a bickering branch
that made her heart nearly stop
when she thought the rope would nip.
How the tyre reddened her leg,
the pain minor to her screams of excitement,
making the hens in the house startle in the dim light,
while the old rooster croaked assurances.

I don't want to be remembered for
shouting at her brother when he chased the rooster
as he tried to get it into the house.
I don't want to be remembered for
giving out to him for wasting grain,
that lay uneaten on the big shed floor,
after all the talk of rats.

I want to be remembered
as the woman who named the blue tit,
that showed her nest boxes newly nailed
and went back down the path with her
when she was afraid the nettles would sting her.

Who let her wear the big black cardigan
even though the sleeves were far too long,
and let her shine the yellow flashlight
into the beams to look for swallows' nests
and waited for her while she tied the gate,
then ran down the hill for home?

If they even remember me at all
it could be summed up in one sentence.
It might just be as simply as this –
'She was that Derry one who rented the Sweeneys' house.'

Robb's Wee House

An Empty Afternoon

Only swallows swipe a white sky bringing promises of rain,
it will empty itself soon. Sitting in the comfort of my car,
I take pleasure in an empty afternoon, where no-one waits for me
or depends on me, or needs me, or marks out the driveway
with heavy tyres. A road going nowhere can only lead to peace.

Rain hits my car like fine gravel, a bluebottle swans in
appreciating the shelter as a September sky sobs above me.
My view is overcrowded with green, bulky branches hold arms
full of rain. Then, like an unexpected visitor, the sun
visits the grass, clouds part like an open curtain bringing
blue. I open the window for air.

The bird table leans painfully to one side, its shoulder heavy
with the weight of fat balls. The birds don't remember me,
how I fed their families, finches peppering the short grass
take my generosity for granted. Later, I climb the field
to the big bay and see three intruders walking the beach.

The world here is mine – this hill, this beach, this field,
the sound of gulls, the air.
Someone claps their hands, hurting the peace and I turn in a huff
cursing under my breath, a herd of sheep part to my walking,
they scatter before their short memories.

The House

The house had a small dark hall
that led you in, it rose slightly to your footfall
as though begrudging you its welcome.
The mat that covered it lay lonely now
for the feel of feet.
A big window laced with cobwebs
cast its eye out to the Swilly, its curtains
hung open to the dark, encouraging
flies to rest in peace on its broad windowsill.
The high mantel loomed over a range
dressed in black, its heart as cold
as an uncovered corpse.
The scraper that scraped it,
the brush that swept its face
and the bucket that carried its soot
sat redundant in the wee tool shed.

The paper cut-out of the naked couple still
stood freezing on the bathroom wall, waiting for a better day.
Along the skirting board woodlice lay on their backs
like exhausted labourers waiting for a lift home.
And the step that led down to the kitchen
always took me by surprise, black beetles
rented cupboard space all summer,
their families called in when it rained, racing across
the floor when lights were on, sheltering in their heavy armour.

It was in the middle of nowhere,
at the end of a road that was going nowhere.
On long winter nights I stayed there alone,
lying awake, listening to the shipping forecast
and the World Service on an old bed-settee,
a gift from someone's shed.
Nervous of intruders, ghosts and earwigs, I lay,
waiting for the morning.
Dozing, just before dawn I would wake
with the taste of dreams still in my mouth,
my nerves resettled with the light of day
till once again I knew the delight of living in that house.

Sailing By

Murder On The Lake

I down my book and rise
to shots echoing across the lake,
I fear for the yellow bittern,
the smew and sightings of the moorhen.
Rushing into a blowing coat,
I slam the sticking door,
it coughs loudly to my leaving.
Evening is hurrying in from Burt,
a heavy sky darkens the lake too early.

Shots drum out again, not sharp but
thunderous their threat is double-barrelled,
too far away to see, they slaughter
dumb ducks for vainglory,
staining the lake with blood.
I call to them on their high *banken*
my mouth spits out words they don't catch,
the wind throws them back at me
they fly off across the lake
where ducks swallow fear in open water.

But my pleas fall on deaf ears,
my heart thunders as I head back along
the Watery Road, carrying their number
plates written on the back of my hand,
for they, that carry tall guns, can see no wrong.

Next day, on the Slab Road
well-intended litter pickers,
assure me it's season for shooting.
'We don't just take life,' he says,
'we pick up rubbish, keeping the place clean, too,
we like to give something back.'
Well, as far as I'm concerned, mister,
you've blood on your hands and it won't wash,
for that's no consolation to a dead duck
floating in pieces on Inch Lake.

The Company Of Swans

In memory of Neil Breslin

From your chimney smoke brushes
the branches of winter foliage,
I watch its grey strokes wave upwards
towards a heavy sky, leaving the scent
of turf hanging in the air.

I hear the overture of swans
busy on the lake
their whiteness cutting cold water,
they call and cry all day long.
Echoes glide over glass

disturbing my silent Sunday.
Only when I go out to fetch wood
does their chorus make me stop,
their wings beat-beat the freezing water
leaving me breathless in their company.

Inch Bank